End Times Prophecies
A Catholic Perspective

Church Prophecy, The Bible, The Mystics, & Saints

By

Michael Freze, S.F.O.

Copyright © 2016 by Michael Freze, S,F.O.
All Rights Reserved

Any Scripture quotations referenced are from the New Revised Standard Version Bible: Catholic Edition (Copyright © 1993) by the Division of Christian Education of the National Council of the Churches of Christ in the U.S.A. Used by permission. All rights reserved.

Table of Contents

Introduction	4
Private Vs. Public Messages	4
Don't Be Afraid To Explore Other Texts	6
How Many Of These Messages Do We Have?	6
Messages From	7
The Blessed Virgin Mary	7
A Need For Careful Discernment	7
Signs of the End Times: Private Prophecies	10
Signs of the End Times: Sacred Scripture	19
The Great Chastisement: Private Prophecies	21
The Great Chastisement: Sacred Scripture	31
Satan and the Antichrist: Private Prophecies	36
Satan and the Antichrist: Sacred Scripture	45
Antichrist	45
Satan	45
The Three Days Darkness: Private Prophecies	48
Examples of Darkness: Sacred Scripture	49
The Great Monarch: Private Prophecies	57
The Great Pope: Private Prophecies	60
The Blessed Virgin Mary: Private Prophecies	62
The Blessed Virgin Mary: Sacred Scripture	65

The End of the Present Age (Private Prophecies)	69
The End of the Present Age: Sacred Scripture	74
The Second Coming of Christ: Private Prophecies	75
The Second Coming of Christ: Sacred Scripture	76
About the Author	78
My Self-Published	80
Religious eBooks In Print	80
Educational Background	83
Television Appearances	84
My YouTube Videos For My National National Appearances	84
Links To My Writing Sites	85

Introduction

Private Vs. Public Messages

Private messages (audible voices or impulses) are received either through **inner locutions** or as private revelations or prophecies through the apparitions of Jesus, Mary, the angels, and the saints. The revelations from Sacred Scripture and both for the benefit of the individual and the world as a whole. Thus, when speaking of messages or revelations from the Bible, we usually refer to those teachings as **public revelations**. Messages received by individual mystics, seers, or saints can be of a private nature, a message for the entire community of faith, or both.

Because they do not represent the collective Sacred Deposit of Faith found in Sacred Scripture and through the traditional teachings of the Church, these messages are to be believed only in terms of human rather than divine faith.

Private revelations can never take the place of or add anything to public revelation already given by the close of the Apostolic era; nor can authentic private revelations teach the faithful anything new about the essential truths of our faith, which are divinely revealed.

However, authentic supernatural messages do echo the words of the Gospel and reflect the true doctrines of the faith. These messages can expand or deepen our understanding of the Gospel and the teachings of the Church. Private revelations may teach us new things about many important issues concerning our faith: particular facts about the life of Jesus, Mary, or the Apostles; a new understanding about various aspects of the interior (spiritual) life; and prophecies about future things not mentioned in the Scriptures and which do not contradict those found in the Bible.

Even of a private message, teaching, warning, or revelation appears to be authentic and benefits a particular person or others, one is still free to believe or not believe any of these messages given after the Bible was completed (or by the close of the Apostolic era). It may be foolish not to believe some of these messages if they appear to be authentic and have inspired or benefited others. Yet it is not demanded one do so.

The closest the Church usually comes to endorsing private revelations is to say that she finds some of them credible and worthy of belief, whereby one may believe with moral certitude that what is taught or encouraged in these messages will bring one closer to God, to the imitation of the ways of Christ, and is consistent with the teachings of the Gospel. One chooses to believe or not believe through the dictates of one's heart, conscience, and reason

One can believe or not believe in these messages by comparing them to the teachings of Sacred Scripture and that of the Fathers of the Church. If messages run contrary or oppose those teachings, the faithful need to use prudent judgment. However, if messages or revelations are new or unique to what we've been given as public revelation and it doesn't run contrary to the universal faith, then one is free to believe or not believe.

A good example is details about the life of Jesus, Mary, the angels, or the saints. Private revelations and messages from these visionaries and mystics may add to our knowledge about personal details that are missing from the Bible. For instance, little is said about Jesus's life until he was baptized and began his ministry. Many mystics have revealed details about these gaps from their various supernatural encounters. The non-canonical Gospels (and many of the early gnostic or deuterocanonical texts) have a great deal to say about the lives of those found in the Bible that the Scriptures don't reveal.

Don't Be Afraid To Explore Other Texts

Although never officially included in the essential public revelations for the universal Church (the canonical texts), they can be of great value in deepening one's understanding of these people, places, and events. A good example is what we've learned since discovering the Dead Sea Scrolls and the Nag Hammadi texts. We now know so much more about the pre-Christian Jewish traditions and the early Christian era by having discovered and translated these works. Furthermore, these texts have enriched our understanding about all the books of the Old Testament and reconfirm their accuracy and authenticity. We even found books that were not known to exist until these finds were made, which greatly expanded our previous known works of many more Jewish texts (including additional books in the Old Testament era).

How Many Of These Messages Do We Have?

How much material do we have of private messages, teachings, and revelations from the mystics and saints? An enormous amount! We have probably more text of all combined prophecies and revelations the past 2,000 years than is even found in the entire Bible! Again, they don't have to be believed; the Sacred Scriptures and the traditional teachings of the Church is enough to satisfy our faith. It would be foolish to disregard all private messages as well, for a wealth of information has expanded our knowledge and understanding of all things related to the Scriptures and the life of the Church since then.

Messages From The Blessed Virgin Mary

A Need For Careful Discernment

In the study of supernatural apparitions that have occurred to specially privileged souls throughout the history of the Church, an obvious fact becomes clear: Marian apparitions outnumber those of any other supernatural or preternatural source (including Jesus, the angels, the saints, and the evil spirit).

It may be argued that the apparitions of our Lord are more numerous than those of Mary. This may be a true fact. But are these cases as well-documented as those involving the Blessed Virgin? We can at least admit that the personal testimonies, eyewitness accounts, and the writings of the faithful concerning Marian apparitions are far greater and more detailed than that of Jesus. Why is this so?

Perhaps one of the answers to such a question involves the very nature of the Blessed Virgin, her special privileges, and her intercessory role among the faithful.

If we look at the information given to us about Mary in Sacred Scripture (as scanty as it is), her special role as Mother of the Church becomes obvious. In John's Gospel, Mary is called at the foot of the cross to be mother of the one whom Jesus loved-John the Evangelist himself: "When Jesus saw his mother, and the disciple whom he loved standing near, he said to his mother, 'Woman, behold your son!' Then he said to the disciple, 'Behold, your mother!' And from that hour the disciple took her to his own home" (Jn 19:26-27).

It is interesting to note that Jesus refers to His Mother, Mary, as "woman" twice in this Gospel-in John 19:26 and in John 2:1-4: "On the third day there was a marriage at Cana in Galilee, and the mother of Jesus was there; Jesus also was invited to the marriage, with his disciples. When the wine failed, the mother of Jesus said to him, 'They have no wine.' And Jesus said to her, 'O woman, what have you to do with me? My hour has not yet come.'" Immediately afterward, Jesus had the disciples fill up their wine jars with water and miraculously turned them into wine (the first of Jesus' miracles in John's Gospel). It was through Mary's motherly concern for her community of faith that Jesus responded accordingly.

Although our Lord can and does appear to others from time to time, it appears that He has commissioned His Mother for the very role she has played since the wedding at Cana; likewise, He has made true the ancient promise that one day a woman would help to intercede against the forces of evil through the coming of her Son, Jesus Christ the Savior (see Gn 3:15).

One only need look at the twelfth chapter of the Book of Revelation to see the role Mary as Queen of Heaven, interceding for humanity in the fight against the powers of darkness. There, the "woman clothed with the sun, with the moon under her feet, and on her head a crown of twelve stars" (Rv 12:1) takes on the forces of Satan and defeats his aggression in union with her Son.

Although hundreds of Marian messages have appeared in the twentieth and twenty-first centuries from dozens of seers, I have chose to focus on just one example that is perhaps the best-known of them all: the apparitions and messages of the Blessed Virgin Mary at Medjugorje in what used to be the country of Yugoslavia. These messages began in 1981 and continue to the present day with at least one of the seers.

Because these Marian apparitions are still occurring as of this date, caution must be exercised until the Church has had time to officially investigate all of these appearances and messages. Although some Church leaders have condemned these visions as a fraud, many others welcome them for the positive messages of hope they bring, the conversions that have occurred, and the ongoing fruits that have manifested in millions around the world.

Although hundreds of Marian messages have appeared in the twentieth and twenty-first centuries from dozens of seers, I have chose to focus on just one example that is perhaps the best-known of them all: the apparitions and messages of the Blessed Virgin Mary at Medjugorje in what used to be the country of Yugoslavia. These messages began in 1981 and continue to the present day with at least one of the seers.

Because these Marian apparitions are still occurring as of this date, caution must be exercised until the Church has had time to officially investigate all of these appearances and messages. Although some Church leaders have condemned these visions as a fraud, many others welcome them for the positive messages of hope they bring, the conversions that have occurred, and the ongoing fruits that have manifested in millions around the world.

Signs of the End Times: Private Prophecies

Let us examination the many Catholic private prophecies that appear to have apocalyptic messages about the end times. In turn, we will also compare these prophecies to those that are recorded in the Sacred Scriptures. Although many of these private revelations of future things are not found explicitly in the Bible ,this lack of scriptural support does not necessarily support a case against their authenticity.

It must be remembered that everything the Lord taught His disciples-and all that the disciples taught about the faith from their own witness or own inspiration-is not found in the Bible: "But there are also many other things which Jesus did; were everyone of them to be written, I suppose that the world itself could not contain the books that would be written" (Jn 21:25).

Knowing this fact, there is nothing to suggest that all private prophecies that are not supported by the sacred texts are false. On the contrary, God continues to speak to His people from age to age; He continues to intervene in salvation history until the end of time: "Lo, I am with you always, to the close of the age" (Mt 28:20).

We can rest assured that Sacred Scripture itself proclaims that voices, visions, and apparitions will occur throughout the history of the Church: "And in the last days it shall be, God declares, that I will pour out my Spirit upon all flesh, and your sons and your daughters shall prophesy, and your young men shall see visions, and your old men shall dream dreams; and I will show wonders in the heaven above and signs on the earth beneath" (Acts 2:17, 19).

On the other hand, just because there will continue to be true prophets and seers from time to time does not shield them from misunderstanding or misinterpreting their supernatural experiences. Thus, the Church wisely teaches that all private revels tions and prophecies be judged in light of human (rather than divine) faith according to the dictates of one's reason, conscience and moral certitude. Good spiritual direction is also an important guide for the seer as well as for any of the faithful who hear about such wonders and messages from a secondary source.

The author has tried to put together a comprehensive section on apocalyptic messages according to various categories that relate to similar themes. Although this provides a unique view of these different messages, there is always a danger of using specific quotes or passages out of their original context. Therefore the author has tried to carefully read the entire context from which these passages were taken.

Sometimes this involved an examination of several paragraphs before and after the quotes order to arrive at such a goal; at other times, it required a deta study of the entire message according to consistent patterns for a particular visionary or seer. If the messages on a specific theme are repeated throughout the text and appear to be similar in meaning, they were generally used in this section.

Likewise, support from Sacred Scripture is given after each of these sections in order to show some kind of consistent pattern or meaning whenever this was possible. This helps to assure that these private revelations are not created out of a vacuum, so to speak, but do have at least some basis of fact in Sacred Scripture. Whether or not the prophecies of the Bible are consistent with our perceptions of the end times is dependent upon careful discernment, prayer, and reflection.

It must be emphasized repeatedly that in no way do these private revelations reflect the teachings, views, or opinions of the magisterium of the Church; nor are they sanctioned or endorsed by the universal Church.

For reasons stated earlier, it is possible that some, many, or even all of these prophecies are exaggerated, misunderstood, misinterpreted, or totally false. On the other hand, it is possible that some or all of these messages are authentic and true. Because the Church rightfully reserves her judgment of such extraordinary phenomena due to the fact that they are based on human (and not divine) faith and reason, let us likewise not ju them one way or another at this point in time. If the Church decides to speak solemnly and with authority on such matters, that time will eventually come.

Although these messages seem very convincing because of their sources and numbers, we must patiently wait to see if their seed will bear fruit. In the meantime, however, for the doubting Thomases of the world, these messages are of a very serious nature. If there is truth to be found in them, a grave risk is taken to discard them out of hand. Thus, one should not dismiss them too prematurely, because the possibility of their literal fulfillment always exists:and this could certainly affect the destiny of us all.

"In the last days false prophets shall be multiplied, and such as corrupt the word, and the sheep shall be changed into wolves, and love into hatred...For men shall hate, and persecute, and betray one another" (Didache and Apostolic Constitutions, 90-100).

"As the end of this world approaches, the condition of human affairs must undergo a change, and through the prevalence of wickedness, become worse" (Lactantius, c. 240-c. 320).

"Priests will act like wolves, care little for spiritual things and live with women. Impiousness, lust and lasciviousness will rule the world. There will be no faith among men, nor peace, nor kindness, nor shame, nor truth" (Lactantius, c. 240-c. 320).

"Falsehood will characterize that class of men who will sit in judgment to pass sentence according to law: between the father and his son, litigations will subsist. The clergy of the holy church will be addicted to pride and injustice. Women will abandon feelings of delicacy, and cohabit with men out of wedlock" (St. Senanus, d. 560).

"Hearken, hearken to what will happen in the latter days of the world! There will be great wars; unjust laws will be enacted; the Church will be despoiled of her property; people will read and write a great deal; but charity and humility will be laughed to scorn, and the common people will believe in false ideas" (St. Columba, d. 597).

"Churches will be empty and dilapidated, priests will have little zeal for souls and pious people will be few. Most people will be given up to all imaginable vices" (St. Gregory the Great, 540-604).

"In the last period Christians will not appreciate the great grace of God...They will be very ungrateful, lead a sinful life, in pride, vanity, unchastity, frivolity, hatred, avarice, gluttony, and many other vices...Many men will doubt whether the Catholic faith is the true and only saving one and whether the Jews are perhaps correct when they still expect the Messiah" (St. Methodius of Constantinople, d. 847).

"Wars and wonders shall befall till the people believe in Christ toward the end of the world" (St. Thomas Becket, 1118-1170).

"The time is coming when princes and peoples will reject the authority of the Pope. Some countries will prefer their own Church rulers to the Pope" (St. Hildegard, 1098-1179).

"Towards the end of the world Israel will commit a terrible crime for which it will suffer death" (Abbot Herman of Lehnin, d. 1300).

"The love of the Incarnate Word as exemplified by His Divine Heart is reserved for the last ages to be made known; so that the world, carried away by follies, may regain a little of the warmth of early Christian charity by learning of the love of the Sacred Heart" (St. Gertrude the Great, 1256-1302).

"There will be a general defection from the Church near the end of the world, especially regarding obedience to Her" (Richard Rolle of Hampole, d. 1349).

"In the days of peace that are to come after the desolation of revolutions and wars, before the end of the world, the Christians will become so lax in their religion that they will refuse to receive the Sacrament of Confirmation, saying 'it is an unnecessary Sacrament' " (St. Vincent Ferrer, 1350-1419).

"The fury of the wars shall last a long time. Whole provinces shall be left naked, and uninhabited, many cities forsaken of people, the nobility slaughtered, principal persons ruined, great changes of kings, commonwealths and rulers" (Blessed Johannes Amadeus de Sylva, d. 1482).

"I understand that devotion to the Sacred Heart is the last effort of His love towards Christians of these latter times, by proposing to them an object and means so calculated to persuade them to love Him" (St. Margaret Mary Alacoque, 1647-1690).

"The return of the Jews to Palestine is the will of God, hence they will have to leave many countries" (Pope Benedict XIV, 1740-1758).

"The Gospel shall be preached freely in the whole world; all the nations of the earth shall fall away from the faith; the Holy Roman Empire shall collapse; Antichrist shall come; Enoch and Elias shall return to preach; the Jews shall return to the Holy Land; the powers of heaven shall be shaken; the stars shall fall from heaven; widespread earthquakes, tidal waves, lightning, wars, famines, and epidemics shall occur" (St. Alphonsus Liguori, 1696-1787).

"The Jews shall return to Palestine and become Christians towards the end of the world" (Venerable Anne Catherine Emmerich, 1774-1824).

"The times are very evil...The entire world will be distressed with afflictions" (The Blessed Virgin Mary to St. Catherine Laboure at Paris, France, 1830).

"Penance! Penance! Penance! Pray for poor sinners. Pray for the world so troubled" (The Blessed Virgin Mary to St. Bernadette Soubirous at Lourdes, France, 1858).

"Supernatural prodigies shall appear in the heavens" (Palma Maria d'Oria, d. 1863).

"During this period, nearly the whole of China shall return to Christianity" (Father Freinademetz, 1906).

"I saw one of my successors taking flight over the bodies of his brethren. He will take refuge in disguise somewhere; and after a short retirement he will die a cruel death. The present wickedness of the world is only the beginning of the sorrows which must take place before the end of the world" (Pope Pius X, 1903-1914).

"The state of the early Christians will come back again; but there will be few men on the earth then! And there will be another magnificent revival of Orders and Congregations" (Pere John Edward Lamy, d. 1931).

"We believe that the present hour is a dread phase of the events foretold by Christ. It seems that darkness is about to fall on the world. Humanity is in the grip of a supreme crisis" (Pope Pius XII, 1939-1958).

"I sometimes read the Gospel passage of the end times and I attest that, at this time, some signs of this end are emerging...Are we close to the end? This we will never know" (Pope Paul VI, 1977).

"At the end of all apparitions in the world, I will leave a great sign in this place and in all those where I have been" (The Blessed Virgin Mary to Patricia Borrero, Cuenca, Ecuador, August, 1988).

"In My love and these times of My special graces I will send you many signs and heavenly apparitions" (Jesus to Jim Singer, Burlington, Ontario, Canada, May, 1989).

"You know by the sign in the heavens which is me that the time is at hand for the instantaneous conversion of the multitude. This I will accomplish through a tremendous outpouring of grace upon the earth given at the hands of God to me for this purpose. This will be the triumph of my Immaculate Heart of which I spoke at Fatima" (The Blessed Virgin Mary to Mariamante, Midwestern United States, 1989).

Signs of the End Times: Sacred Scripture

"And this gospel of the kingdom will be preached throughout the whole world, as a testimony to all nations; and then the end will come" (Mt 24:14).

"For many will come in my name, saying, 'I am the Christ,' and they will lead many astray" (Mt 24:5).

"And you will hear of wars and rumors of wars; see that you are not alarmed; for this must take place, but the end is not yet" (Mt 24:6).

"For nation will rise against nation, and kingdom against kingdom, and there will be famines and earthquakes in various places: all this is but the beginning of the sufferings" (Mt 24:7-8).

"Then they will deliver you up to tribulation, and put you to death; and you will be hated by all nations for my name's sake" (Mt 24:9).

":Many will fall away, and betray one another, and hate one another" (Mt 24:10).

"And many false prophets will arise and lead many astray" (Mt 24:11).

"Because wickedness is multiplied, most men's love will grow cold" (Mt 24:12).

"So when you see the desolating sacrilege spoken of by the prophet Daniel, standing the holy place (let the reader understand), then let those who are in Judea flee to the mountains" (Mt 24:15-16).

"For false Christs and false prophets will arise and show great signs and wonders, so as to lead astray, if possible, even the elect" (Mt 24:24).

"Jerusalem will be trodden down by the Gentiles, until the times of the Gentiles are fulfilled" (Lk 21:24).

"And there will be signs in sun and moon and stars, and upon the earth distress of nations in perplexity at the roaring of the sea and the waves, men fainting with fear and with foreboding of what is coming on the world" (Lk 21:25-26).

The Great Chastisement: Private Prophecies

"Men and people have risen up against the other. War, war, war-civil war and foreign war. What frightening onsets. Everything is mourning and death; famine reigns in the fields" (Premol, d.496).

"Dreadful plagues will come upon all the race of Adam" (St. Senanus, d. 560).

Dreadful storms and hurricanes shall afflict them. Numberless diseases shall then prevail" (St. Columba, d. 597).

"During the last persecution of the Holy Roman Church, there will sit upon the throne, Peter the Roman, who will feed the sheep amid great tribulations, and when these are passed, the City of Seven Hills (Rome) will be utterly destroyed, and the awful Judge will then judge the people" (St. Malachy of Ireland, 1095-1148).

"Toward the end of the world, mankind will be purified through sufferings. This will be true especially of the clergy, who will be robbed of all property" (St. Hildegard, 1098-1179).

"Before the comet comes, many nations, the good excepted, will be scourged with want and famine. The comet by its tremendous pressure, will force much out of the ocean and flood many countries, causing much want and many plagues. All sea coast cities will be fearful and many of them will be destroyed by tidal waves, and most living creatures will be killed and even those who escape will die from a horrible disease" (St. Hildegard, 1098-1179).

"The nations will be in wars for four years and a great ps the world will be destroyed. All the sects will vanish. The capital of the world will fall" (Werdin d'Otrante, thirteenth century).

"The sufferings of the Church will be much greater than any previous time in her history (Brother John of the Cleft Rock, d.1340).

"The earth shall be deluged with the blood of its inhabitants. Her children, armed with iron, shall perish by the sword. Her innumerable calamities, says the Lord, shall not appease my wrath. My right hand shall be lifted up against the people; the power that will oppress them shall be my instrument of indignation against them, and against other nations" (Father Jerome Votin, d. 1420).

"The Church will be punished because the majority of her members, high and low, will become so perverted. The Church will sink deeper and deeper until she will at last seem to be extinguished, and the succession of Peter and the other Apostles to have expired. But, after this, she will be victoriously exalted in the sight of all doubters" (St. Nicholas of Flue, 1417-1487).

"The great chastisement will come when carriages go without horses and many accidents fill the world with woe. It will come when thoughts are flying around the earth in the twinkling of all eye, when long tunnels are made for horseless machines, when man can fly in the air and ride under the sea, when ships are wholly made of metal, when fire and water great marvels do, when even the poor can read books, and when many taxes are levied for war" (Mother Shipton, sixteenth century).

"Many cities and villages shall be in ruins, with the deaths of an innumerable quantity of bad and good men" (St. Vincent de Paul, 1580-1660).

"An unusual chastisement of the human race will take place towards the end of the world" (Venerable Mary of Agreda, d. 1665).

"God will punish the world when men have devised marvelous inventions that will lead them to forgetting God. They will have horseless carriages, and they will fly like the birds" (Blessed Rembordt, eighteenth century).

"Before the great combat the wicked shall be masters. They will perpetrate all the evils in their power, but not so much as they desire, because they shall not have the time. Good and faithful Catholics, less in number, shall be on the point of being annihilated, but a stroke from heaven shall save them" (Sister Marianne, d. 1804).

"Religious shall be persecuted, priests shall be massacred, the churches shall be closed, but only for a short time; the Holy Father shall be obliged to abandon Rome" (Blessed Anna Maria Taigi, d. 1837).

"All over Europe there will rage terrible civil wars. God has long been patient with the corruption of morals...He will destroy half of mankind. The poor will be rich and rich poor" (Brother Louis Rocco, d. 1840).

"Before the triumph of the Church comes, God will first take vengeance on the wicked, pecially the godless. It will be a new judgment; the like has never been seen before, and it will be universal. It will be so terrible that those who outlive it will imagine that they are the only ones spared" (Father Bernard Maria Clausi, O.F.M., d. 1849).

"I see the Lord as He will be scourging the world, and chastising it in a fearful manner so that few men and women will remain. The monks will have to leave their monasteries, and the nuns will be driven from their convents, especially in Italy .... The Holy Church will be persecuted...Unless people obtain pardon through their prayers, the time will come when they will see the sword and death, and Rome will be without a shepherd" (Abbess Maria Steiner, d. 1862).

"Many priests have lost their fervor for the honor of God and the salvation of souls. Their hearts hang too much on the phantoms of this life. God will, by chastisements, cure them thereof and so thereby change them. In many religious houses the spirit of poverty and simplicity is forgotten" (Mother Alphonse Eppinger, d. 1867).

"All states will be shaken by war and civil conflict. During a darkness lasting three days the people given to evil ways will perish so that only one-fourth of mankind will survive. The clergy, too, will be greatly reduced in number, as most of them will die in defense of the faith or of their country" (Sister Mary of Jesus Crucified of Pau, d. 1878).

"The ocean will cast its foaming waves over the land; the earth will be changed to an immense cemetery; the corpses of the wicked and the just will cover the face of the earth. The famine that follows will be great. All vegetation will be destroyed as well a! three-fourths of the human race. The crisis will come all of a sudden and chastisement will be world wide" (Marie-Julie Jahenny of Coyault, France, d. 1941).

"The human race will have to go through a great storm that will sharpen divisions among men and reduce their plan to ashes" (Berthe Petit, 1870-1943).

"Clouds with lightning flashes of fire in the sky and a tempest of fire shall fall upon the world. This terrible scourge, never before seen in this history of humanity, will last seventy hours" (The Blessed Mother to Mother Elena Aiello of Calabria, Italy, April 1, 1947).

"Too many people keep on piercing the Heart of my Son. If they do not repent, God will send this world terrible retribution and catastrophe" (The Blessed Virgin Mary to Sister Teresa Musco of Italy, July 11, 1950).

"The times will come when the spiritual and moral deterioration of the shepherds of my Son's flock will be a matter of public knowledge. Spiritual growth will become very difficult for the children of God and further times will come when such growth will seem almost impossible. Beware, my children, because indifference and confusion will prevail along the way, and throughout the world" (The Blessed Virgin Mary to Barrio Rincon, Sabana Grande, Puerto Rico, 1953).

"The furies of hell rage now. The chastisement of God is inevitable" (Therese Neumann, 1898-1962).

"Tell all nations that God has spoken by the mouth of His servant. He has revealed to her that the Great Tribulation is near, for she has seen that the Sign of the Son of Man which rises in the East is forthwith in the West...this Sign of the Son of Man is the Lord's Cross" (Madeleine of Dozule, France, 1974).

"A terrible flaming scourge is prepared. It will purify the world of the many and grievous sins which envelope it like a dark obfuscation" (The Blessed Virgin Mary to Mother Elena Patriarca Leonardi at Rome, Italy, March 2,1975).

"If you do not change, you will shorten the time before the third world war" (The Blessed Virgin Mary to Bernard Martinez of Cuapa, Nicaragua, 1980).

"The heavenly Father will send a terrible punishment over the whole world of mankind if people do not repent and change their lives: a punishment that will be more terrible than the great flood; a punishment the world has never experienced. Fire will fall from heaven and destroy the larger part of mankind and will not spare priests and lay people. The survivors will suffer so much that they will envy the dead" (The Blessed Virgin Mary to Sister Agnes Sasagawa at Akita, Japan, 1973-1982).

"Repent, because the Great Purification is coming" (The Blessed Virgin Mary to Theresa of Vietnam, January 25, 1982).

"Today many persons go to Hell. God permits his children to suffer in Hell due to the fact that they have committed grave unpardonable sins. Those who are in Hell, no longer have a chance to know a better lot" (The Blessed Virgin Mary to the seers of Medjugorje, Yugoslavia, July 25, 1982).

"I have prayed; the punishment has been softened. Repeat prayers and fasting reduce punishments from God, but it is not possible to avoid entirely the chastisement" (The Blessed Virgin Mary to Mirjana Dragicevic, Medjugorje, Yugoslavia, November 6, 1982).

"Mirjana, I have chosen you, I have confided in you everything that is essential. I have also shown you many terrible things. You must now bear it all with courage" (The Blessed Virgin Mary to Mirjana Dragicevic, Medjugorje, Yugoslavia, December 25, 1982).

"A great castigation for humanity is near" (The Blessed Virgin Mary to stigmatist Miguel Angel Poblete of Penablanca, Chile, June 12, 1983).

"The Lord is now gathering the good against the evil. The world would long ago have been destroyed but the soul of the world would not allow this. As the soul preserves the life of the body, so do Christians preserve the life of the world. God needs fervent and constant sons. You shall go through the ways of the world and give witness, and in the end God will punish the apostates because only through this punishment will God be able to bring man back to sound reason. And when the faith and love shall be reborn, Satan will begin a new persecution of the Christians. Times of persecution will begin, of priests and the faithful. The world will be divided into the messengers of God and messengers of Antichrist. After the great revelations of the Virgin Mary, renewal of love of Christ will begin" (St. Michael the Archangel to Josyp Terelya, Vladimir Prison, Russia, July 17, 1983).

"The world lives amidst very strong tensions. It is on the edge of catastrophe...Tell the whole world; tell it without delay, that I ardently wish conversion. Be converted, do not wait. I will ask my Son that He not chastise the world. Convert yourselves, renounce everything, and be ready for everything" (The Blessed Virgin Mary to the seers of Medjugorje, Yugoslavia, 1984).

"I have come for the sake of my Son. I cannot restrain His hand much longer. Prayer is the best weapon you have. The devil is strong with those who fear him and weak with those who despise him" (The Blessed Virgin Mary to Mary Casey, Inchigeela, Ireland, 1985).

"She showed me again the terrible burning of the world with such fire and desolation. There were screams and people stretching their hands out of the fire, calling for help. The pain and the agony were horrible" (The Blessed Virgin Mary to Patricia of the Divine Innocence [from England], July 18, 1985).

"Pray for Russia. Pray for the lost Russian nation. If Russia does not accept Christ the King, the Third World War cannot be averted" (The Blessed Virgin Mary to Josyp Terelya, Hrushiv, Ukraine, May 9, 1987).

"The world must behave. The world must change. A great catastrophe will happen to the world. Tell them to hurry. This is a command from God. The messages here are the messages of Medjugorje" (The Blessed Virgin Mary to Beulah Lynch of Bessbrook, Northern Ireland, June, 1987).

"In this period of ten years there will come to its culmination that purification which, for a number of years now, you have been living through and therefore the sufferings will become greater for all. . .In this period of ten years there will come to completion the time of the great tribulation, which has been foretold to you in Holy Scripture, before the second coming of Jesus" (The Blessed Virgin Mary to Father Stefano Gobbi, September 18, 1988).

"The chastisement shall be a result of misbelief, lack of love, lack of faith, lack of respect and from a lack of your mercy! I tell you, if you change your heart and live what I tell you, goodness, purity, and beauty can be restored by destroying evil now. You have the power to destroy evil if you all focus on Me and allow Me to live in you. You can prevent the chastisement from My Father!" (Jesus to Gianna Talone, Scottsdale, Arizona, June 5,1989).

"If there is no change or improvement of life, you will succumb under fire: war and death. This is why, again, in this century, my Divine Son arises" (The Blessed Virgin Mary to Maria Esperanza Bianchini, Betania, Venezuela, 1992).

"My angels are touching the earth. They haven't struck. Mark what I say: They haven't struck" (Jesus to Beulah Lynch, Bessbrook, Northern Ireland, January 12, 1992).

The Great Chastisement: Sacred Scripture

"For then there will be great tribulation, such as has not been from the beginning of the world until now, no, and never will be. And if those days had not been shortened, no human being would be saved; but for the sake of the elect those days will be shortened" (Mt 24:21-22).

"Nation will rise against nation, and kingdom against kingdom; there will be great earthquakes, and in various places famines and pestilences; and there will be terrors and great signs from heaven. But before all this they will lay their hands on you and persecute you, delivering you up to the synagogues and prisons, and you will be brought before kings and governors for my name's sake" (Lk 21:10-12).

"But when you see Jerusalem surrounded by armies, then know that its desolation has come near. Then let those who are in Judea flee to the mountains, and let those who are inside the city depart, and let not those who are out in the country enter it; for these are days of vengeance, to fulfil all that is written. Alas for those who are with child and for those who give suck in those days! For great distress shall be upon the earth and wrath upon this people; they will fall by the edge of the sword, and be led captive among the nations" (Lk 21:20-24).

"And there will be signs in sun and moon and stars, and upon the earth distress of nations in perplexity at the roaring of the sea and the waves, men fainting with fear and with foreboding of what is coming on the world; for the powers of heaven will be shaken" (Lk 21:25-26).

"And out came another horse, bright red; its rider was permitted to take peace from the earth, so that men should slay one another" (Rv 6:4).

"And I saw, and behold, a black horse, and its rider had balance in his hand; and I heard what seemed to be a voice in the midst of the four living creatures saying, 'A quart of wheat for a denarius, and three quarts of barley for a denarius' " (Rv 6:5-6).

"And I saw, and behold, a pale horse, and its rider's name was Death, and Hades followed him; and they were given power over a fourth of the earth, to kill with sword and with famine and with pestilence and by wild beasts of the earth" (Rv 6:8).

"When he opened the fifth seal, I saw under the altar the souls of those who had been slain for the word of God and for the witness they had borne; they cried out with a loud voice, "O Sovereign Lord, holy and true, how long before thou wilt judge and avenge our blood on those who dwell upon the earth?"' (Rv 6:9-10).

"There was a great earthquake; and the sun became black as sackcloth, the full moon became like blood, and the stars of the sky fell to the earth as the fig tree sheds its winter fruit when shaken by a gale; the sky vanished like a scroll that is rolled up, and every mountain and island was removed from its place" (Rv 6:12-14).

"Then the kings of the earth and the great men and the generals and the rich and the strong, and everyone, slave and free, hid in the caves and among the rocks of the mountains, calling to the mountains and rocks, 'Fall on us and hide us from the face of him who is seated on the throne, and from the wrath of the Lamb; for the great day of their wrath has come, and who can stand before it?' " (Rv 6:15-17).

"The first angel blew his trumpet, and there followed hail and fire, mixed with blood, which fell on the earth; and a third of the earth was burnt up, and a third of the trees were burnt up, and all green grass was burnt up" (Rv 8:7).

"A third of the sea became blood, a third of the living creatures in the sea died, and a third of the ships were destroyed" (Rv 8:9).

"A great star fell from heaven, blazing like a torch, and it fell on a third of the rivers and on the fountains of water. The name of the star is Wormwood. A third of the waters became wormwood, and many men died of the water, because it was made bitter" (Rv 8:10-11).

"A third of the sun was struck, and a third of the moon, and a third of the stars, so that a third of their light was darkened; a third of the day was kept from shining, and likewise a third of the night" (Rv 8:12).

"Then from the smoke came locusts on the earth, and they were given power like the power of scorpions of the earth; they were told not to harm the grass of the earth or any green growth or any tree, but only those of mankind who have not the seal of God upon their foreheads; they were allowed to torture them for five months, but not to kill them, and their torture was like the torture of a scorpion, when it stings a man. And in those days men will seek death and will not find it; they will long to die, and death will fly from them" (Rv 9:3-6).

"And this was how I saw the horses in my vision: the riders wore breastplates the color of fire and of sapphire and of sulphur, and the heads of the horses were like lions' heads, and fire and smoke and sulphur issued from their mouths. By these three plagues a third of mankind was killed, by the fire and smoke an sulphur issuing from their mouths. For the power of the horses is in their mouths and in their tails; their tails are like serpents, with heads, and by means of them they wound" (Rv 9:17-19).

"For it is given over to the nations, and they will trample over the holy city for forty-two months" (Rv 11:2).

"There was a great earthquake, and a tenth of the city fell; seven thousand people were killed in the earthquake, and the rest were terrified and gave glory to the God of heaven" (Rv 11:13).

"There were flashes of lightning, loud noises, peals of thunder, an earthquake, and heavy hail" (Rv 11:19).

"Fear God and give him glory, for the hour of his judgment has come" (Rv 14:7).

"Fallen, fallen is Babylon the great, she who made all nations drink the wine of her impure passion" (Rv 14:8).

Satan and the Antichrist: Private Prophecies

"For this is what the prophets Enoch and Elias will preach: "Believe not the enemy who is to come and be seen; for he is an adversary and corrupter and son of perdition, and deceives you" (St. Hippolytus, d. c. 235).

"After the birth of Antichrist, most people will possess some thing that they stole, they will be greedy, godless, selfish, hard hearted. Justice will have disappeared from the earth, man will neither know law, order nor discipline. Murderers and robbers will fill the whole world...The time of nation fighting against nation will occur after the birth of Antichrist, and then the world shall be despoiled of beauty through the destruction of men" (Lactantius, c. 240-c. 320) .

"Antichrist will teach that Christ was an imposter and not the real Son of God" (St. Hilary of Poitiers, d. c. 367).

"Antichrist will use worldly goods as bait. He will entice many Christians with money and goods to apostatize. He will give them free land, riches, honor and power. The devil will help him find all the hidden treasures of the world, even those at the bottom of the oceans" (St. Ephrem, d. c. 375).

"Antichrist will exceed in malice, perversity, lust, wickedness, impiety, and heartless cruelty and barbarity all men that have ever disgraced human nature...He shall through his great power, deceit and malice, succeed in decoying or forcing to his worship two thirds of mankind; the remaining third part of men will most steadfastly continue true to the faith and worship of Jesus Christ" (St. Cyril of Jerusalem, d. 386).

"Antichrist shall work a thousand prodigies on earth. He will make the blind see, the deaf hear, the lame walk, the dead rise, so that even the elect, if possible, shall be deceived by his magical arts. He shall seduce many credulous persons through his deceitful errors" (St. Zenobius, d. c. 390).

"The world will be faithless and degenerate after the birth of Antichrist" (St. John Chrysostom, 347-407).

"Antichrist will be born near Babylon. He will gain support of many with gifts and money. He will sell himself to the devil and thereafter will have no guardian angel or conscience" (St. Jerome, 342-420).

"After some considerable time fervor shall cool, iniquity shall abound, and moral corruption shall become worse than ever, which shall bring upon mankind the last and worse persecution of Antichrist, and the end of the world" (St. Caesar of Arles, d. 543).

"During the three-and-one-half-years-reign of Antichrist, God will send Enoch and Elias to help the Christians" (St. Benedict of Nursia, d. 547).

"After the birth of Antichrist most of mankind will be such as corrupt the word; and the sheep shall be changed into godless or fallen into heresy" (St. Gregory the Great, 540-604).

"The just God will give Lucifer and all his devils power to come on earth and tempt his godless creatures" (St. Methodius [with St. Cyril], d. 884).

"Antichrist will rule the world from Jerusalem which he will make into a magnificent city" (St. Anselm, d. 1109).

"After the birth of Antichrist heretics will preach their false doctrines undisturbed, resulting in Christians having doubt about their holy Catholic faith" (St. Hildegard, 1098-1179).

"Although men will be terrified by the signs appearing about the judgment day, yet before those signs begin to appear the wicked will think themselves to be in peace and security after the death of Antichrist and before the coming of Christ, seeing that the world is not at once destroyed as they thought hitherto" (St. Thomas Aquinas, 1225-1274).

"The time of Antichrist will be near when the means of injustice will overflow and when wickedness has grown to immense proportions, when the Christians love heresies and the unjust trample underfoot the servants of God" (St. Bridget of Sweden, 1303-1373).

"When the false prophet, the precursor of Antichrist comes, all who are not confirmed will apostatize, while those who are confirmed will stand firm in the faith, and only a few will renounce Christ" (St. Vincent Ferrer, 1350-1419).

"There shall be signs of the sun and moon where there shall be created a man stronger than any prince, and he shall renew the face of the earth. At this time Antichrist shall have been trodden under foot and all the world shall enjoy the faith and peace of the Most High" (St. John Capistran, 1386-1456).

"At the time when Antichrist is about twenty years old, most of the world will have lost the faith" (Bernard de Busto, d. 1490).

"Antichrist will live fifty-five and one-half years, that is, 666 months" (Venerable Bartholomew Holzhauser, d. 1658).

"When the world will be drowned in terrible vices, Satan and all his devils will be let loose so that they may pave the way for the godless Antichrist to attain world dominion and final persecution" (Venerable Mary of Agreda, d. 1665).

"After the birth of Antichrist the people of the world will b very wicked and Godless. People of real virtue will be very scarce. Pastors in many places will neglect the service of God, and live with women. Even the religious will crave for worldly things. The churches will be dreary and empty like deserted barns...at the time when Antichrist is about twenty years of age the whole world will be without faith, subjects will be oppressed by rulers and others in authority. In every period of tribulation God aided His Church, and He will do it at the time before the coming of Antichrist" (Dionysius of Luxembourg, d. 1682).

"I was told, if I remember right, that Satan will be unchained for a time fifty or sixty years before the year of Christ 2,000" (Venerable Anne Catherine Emmerich, 1774-1824).

"Nothing on earth shall be spared. God will allow the demons to strike with death those impious men because they gave themselves up to the infernal powers and had formed with them a compact against the Catholic Church" (Elizabeth Canori-Mora, d. 1825).

"The air will be infested by demons, who will appear under all sorts of hideous forms. Whole nations will join the Church shortly before the reign of Antichrist. These conversions will be amazing" (Blessed Anna Maria Taigi, d. 1837).

"In most people respect for God has disappeared both in public and in private life. They even go so far as to attempt to obliterate even the memory of God. When we consider these facts you must really feel that such wickedness is only the beginning of those evils which are to come before the end of the world, and that the Son of Perdition of whom the Apostles speak, is already among us" (Pope Pius X, 1903-1914).

"It is a spectacle so appalling that one might see already the dawn of the beginning of sorrows that will bring 'the man of sin' arising against all which is called God and is honored by worship" (Pope Pius XI, 1922-1939).

"Lucifer is playing his last card; he thinks the game is in his hands, in which he is mistaken" (Pere John Edward Lamy, d. 1931).

"Satan prowls around you, sets traps for you. He tries to divide you, you the seers, to plant discord among you" (The Blessed Virgin Mary to Mirjana Dragicevic, Medjugorje, Yugoslavia, as told to Father Janko Bubalo in 1981).

"A great battle is about to take place. A battle between my Son and Satan. Human souls are at stake" (The Blessed Virgin to Marija Pavlovic, Medjugorje, Yugoslavia, August 2, 1981).

"The Devil tries to reign over people. He takes everything into his hands, but the force of God is more powerful, and God will conquer" (The Blessed Virgin Mary to Vicka Ivankovic, Medjugorje, Yugoslavia, September 2, 1981).

"The Devil is trying to conquer us. Do not permit him. Keep the faith, fast and pray" (The Blessed Virgin Mary to Jakov Colo, Medjugorje, Yugoslavia, November 16,1981).

"Excuse me for this, but you must realize that Satan exists. One day he appeared before the throne of God and asked permission to submit the Church to a period of trial. God gave him permission to try the Church for one century. This century is under the power of the Devil, but when the secrets confided to you come to pass, his power will be destroyed. Even now he is beginning to lose his power and has become aggressive. He is destroying marriages, creating division among priests and is responsible for obsessions and murder" (The Blessed Virgin Mary to Mirjana Dragicevic, Medjugorje, Yugoslavia, 1982).

"Be prudent because the Devil tempts all those who have made a resolution to consecrate themselves to God, most particularly, those people. He will suggest to them that they are praying very much, they are fasting too much, that they must be like other young people and go in search of pleasures. Have them not listen to him, nor obey him" (The Blessed Virgin Mary in a locution to Jelena Vasilj of Medjugorje, Yugoslavia, June 16, 1983).

"Be on your guard. This period is dangerous for you. The Devil is trying to lead you astray from your way. Those who give themselves to God will be the objects of attacks" (The Blessed Virgin Mary in a locution to Jelena Vasilj of Medjugorje, Yugoslavia, July 26, 1983).

"Dear children, in these days, Satan wants to destroy all my plans. Pray with me so that his design will not be realized" (The Blessed Virgin Mary in a message for the parish of Medjugorje, Yugoslavia, July 12, 1984).

"The hour has come when the demon is authorized to act with all his force and power. The present hour is the hour of Satan" (The Blessed Virgin Mary to Mirjana Dragicevic, Medjugorje, Yugoslavia, 1985).

"Dear children! Satan is manifesting himself in this parish in a particular way these days. Pray, dear children, that God's plan be carried out, and that every work of Satan be turned to the glory of God" (The Blessed Virgin Mary to Marija Pavlovic, Medjugorje, Yugoslavia, February 7,1985).

"I urge you to ask everyone to pray the rosary. With the rosary you will overcome all the troubles which Satan is trying to inflict on the Catholic Church" (The Blessed Virgin Mary to Marija Pavlovic, Medjugorje, Yugoslavia, June 25, 1985).

"These are my last apparitions to mankind. With the events which are preparing themselves, and which are near, the power of Satan still holds but will be withdrawn from him. The present century has been under his power. Now that he is conscious of losing the battle, he is becoming more aggressive" (The Blessed Virgin Mary to Boa Nova at Medjugorje, Yugoslavia, 1986).

"The days until the tempest are numbered. Lucifer has been loosed from his fiery pit ....I will send a great sign in the skies for you, time is very short. Judas Iscariot has been raised from his sleep-he is amongst you-his evil will have no precedent. Many, many lives will be taken. Men will call out to die. Cling to me and fear not" (The Blessed Virgin Mary to Paul of the Blue Mountains in South Wales, Australia, February 1 and 20, 1986).

"Lucifer is losing strength. To maintain himself on the throne of darkness he began portraying himself as repentant, but this is not true. Lucifer is cunning and clever. He is preparing a great deception for all of God's creation, and especially for the people of God. For a short time a godless kingdom shall maintain itself from one end of the earth to the other" (The Blessed Virgin Mary to Josyp Terelya, Hrushiv, Ukraine, May 9,1987).

"All I tell you is in Sacred Scripture. A false prophet exists who will entangle (my little souls) saying that he is God, but he is from the blood of the demon. He will betray the Father. And the one who has the heart and wisdom will realize that he carries the number of the beast, 666, on his right hand. Satan is set loose to touch my little ones, but I am that woman whom the Father announced, who will crush the head of the serpent that is Satan" (The Blessed Virgin Mary to Patricia Borrero, Cuenca, Ecuador, 1990).

"Satan is strong and wishes not only to destroy human life but also nature and the planet on which you live" (The Blessed Virgin Mary to Marija Pavlovic, Medjugorje, Yugoslavia, January, 1991).

"Satan is strong and wants to sweep away plans of peace and joy and make you think that my Son is not strong in his decisions" (The Blessed Virgin Mary to Marija Pavlovic, Medjugorje, Yugoslavia, August 25, 1991).

"The influence of the Prince of Darkness is all around you. Arm yourselves with the Rosary. My Church will be shaken, even to its foundation. My children who want to be saved must repent" (The Blessed Virgin Mary to Christina Gallagher, Carns, Ireland, 1992).

Satan and the Antichrist: Sacred Scripture

Antichrist

"And from the time that the continual burnt offering is taken away, and the abomination that makes desolate is set up, there shall be a thousand two hundred and ninety days" (Dn 12:11).

"Children, it is the last hour; and as you have heard that Antichrist is coming, so now many antichrists have come; therefore we know that it is the last hour" (Jn 2:18).

"Who is the liar but he who denies that Jesus is the Christ? This is the antichrist, he who denies the Father and the Son" (Jn 2:22).

"Every spirit which does not confess Jesus is not of God. This is the spirit of antichrist, of which you heard that it was coming, and now it is in the world already" (1 Jn 4:3).

"For many deceivers have gone out into the world, men who will not acknowledge the coming of Jesus Christ in the flesh; such a one is the deceiver and the antichrist" (2 Jn 1:7).

Satan

"Through the devil's envy death entered the world, and those who belong to his party experience it" (Wis 2:24).

"I saw Satan fall like lightning from heaven" (Lk 10:18).

"The coming of the lawless one by the activity of Satan will be with all power and with pretended signs and wonders, and with all wicked deception for those who are to perish, because they refused to love the truth and so be saved" (2 Thes 2:9-10).

"And the fifth angel blew his trumpet, and I saw a star fallen from heaven to earth, and he was given the key the key of the shaft of the bottomless pit" (Rv 9:1).

"Now war arose in heaven, Michael and his angels fighting against the dragon; and the dragon and his angels fought, but they were defeated and there was no longer any place for them in heaven. And the great dragon was thrown down, that ancient serpent, who is called the Devil and Satan, the deceiver of the whole world-he was thrown down to the earth, and his angels were thrown down with him" (Rv 12:7-9).

"Woe to you, earth and sea, for the devil has come down to you in great wrath, because he knows that his time is short!" (Rv 12:12).

"And I saw a beast rising out of the sea, with ten horns and seven heads, with ten diadems upon its horns and a blasphemous name upon its heads. And the beast that I saw was like a leopard, its feet were like a bear's, and its mouth was like a lion's mouth. And to it the dragon gave his power and his throne and great authority. One of its heads seemed to have a mortal wound, but its mortal wound was healed, and the whole earth followed the beast with wonder. Men worshiped the dragon, for he had given his authority to the beast, and they worshiped the beast, saying, 'Who is like the beast, and who can fight against it?' And the beast was given a mouth uttering haughty and blasphemous words, and it was allowed to exercise authority for forty-two months" (Rv 13:1-5).

"This calls for wisdom: let him who has understanding reckon the number of the beast, for it is a human number, its number is six hundred and sixty-six" (Rv 13:18).

"The sixth angel poured his bowl on the great river Euphrates, and its water was dried up, to prepare the way for the kings from the east. And I saw, issuing from the mouth of the dragon and from the mouth of the beast and from the mouth of the false prophet, three foul spirits like frogs; for they are demonic spirits, performing signs, who go abroad to the kings of the whole world, to assemble them for battle on the great day of God the Almighty. . .And they assembled them at the place which is called in Hebrew Armageddon" (Rv 16:12-14,16).

"Then I saw an angel coming down from heaven, holding in his hand the key of the bottomless pit and a great chain. And he seized the dragon, that ancient serpent, who is the Devil and Satan, and bound him for a thousand years, and threw him in the pit, and shut it and sealed it over him, that he should deceive the nations no more, till the thousand years were ended. After that he must loosed for a little while" (Rv 20:1-3).

The Three Days Darkness: Private Prophecies

"God will ordain two punishments: One, in the form of wars, revolutions and other evils, will originate on earth; the other will be sent from heaven. There shall come over all the earth an intense darkness lasting three days and three nights. Nothing will be visible and the air will be laden with pestilence, which will claim principally but not exclusively the enemies of religion. During this darkness artificial light will be impossible. Only blessed candles can be lighted and will afford illumination. He who out of curiosity opens his window to look out or leaves his house will fall dead on the spot. During these three days the people should remain in their homes, pray the Rosary and beg God for mercy" (Blessed Anna Maria Taigi, d. 1837).

"There will be destruction of impenitent persecutors of the Church during the three days darkness. To him who outlives the darkness and fear of the three days, it will seem as if he were alone on earth because the world will be covered everywhere with carcasses" (St. Caspar del Bufalo, d. 1837).

"There shall be a three days darkness, during which the atmosphere will be infected by innumerable devils, who shall cause the death of large multitudes of unbelievers and wicked men. Blessed candles alone shall be able to give light and preserve the faithful Catholics from this impending dreadful scourge" (Palma Maria d'Oria, d. 1863).

"There will come three days of continual darkness. The blessed candles of wax alone will give light during the horrid darkness. One candle will last for three days, but in the houses of the god less they will not give light. During those three days the demons will appear in abominable and horrible forms; they will make the air resound with shocking blasphemies" (Marie-Julie Jahenny of Coyault, France, d. 1941).

"My child, I have decided to show my power by three days and three nights of darkness. Mankind's sins increase day after day" (Theresa of Vietnam, 1977).

"Take care to guard your blessed objects, my children. They will serve you when the day of darkness comes. During those three days and those three nights, those objects will shine, my child. They will shine no matter where they are" (The Blessed Virgin Mary to stigmatist Amparo Cuevas of El Escorial, Spain, November 25, 1984).

Examples of Darkness: Sacred Scripture

"Then the Lord said to Moses, 'Stretch out your hand toward heaven that there may be darkness over the land of Egypt, a darkness to be felt.' So Moses stretched out his hand toward heaven, and there was thick darkness in all the land of Egypt for three days; they did not see one another, nor did any rise from his place for three days; but all the people of Israel had light where they dwelt" (Ex 10:21-23).

Author's comment: Note that even near the beginning of Sacred Scripture, God punished the unbelievers and idolaters with a three-day darkness. Interestingly, he allows the faithful community of Israel to see through the darkness He ordains. This closely parallels the private prophecies predicting that a three-day darkness is coming to chastise the world for its sins (as God had done to Pharaoh and his Egyptians). Also, there is a similar grace predicted for all the faithful Christians: If they keep a blessed candle lit during this time of tribulation, God promises to spare them of such a fate (as the faithful remnant of Israel were spared of such darkness before).

"The LORD will smite you with madness and blindness and confusion of mind; and you shall grope at noonday, as the blind grope in darkness" (Dt 28:28-29).

Author's comment: Again God uses darkness as a punishment for those who disobey His laws and who transgress the holy covenant.

"He will guard the feet of his faithful ones; but the wicked shall be cut off in darkness" (1 Sm 2:9).

Author's comment: Here we see that the Lord guards His faithful ones (through the light of blessed candles as stated in private prophecies) and chastises the godless with a period of darkness. Although these symbols of darkness in Scripture may represent a dark night of the spirit or senses, nevertheless it is a darkness just the same - a total separation from God.

"Let that day be darkness! May God above not seek it, nor light shine upon it. Let gloom and deep darkness claim it. Let clouds dwell upon it; let the blackness of the day terrify it. That night-let thick darkness seize it!" (Jb 3:4-6).

Author's comment: Here the troubled Job bewails his birth, sorry for his past offenses against God. In a similar way, the apocalyptic prophecies warn of damnation for those who do not repent and live the faith that God demands of all.

"They grope in the dark without light; and he makes them stagger like a drunken man" (12:25).

Author's comment: Compare this prophetic utterance of Job with the words of St. Caspar del Bufalo mentioned earlier.

"He is thrust from light into darkness, and driven out of the world" (Jb 18: 18).

Author's comment: Job is describing the lot of the wicked. Compare this warning of damnation for the "wicked" to that of the words of Palma Maria d'Oria cited earlier.

"What does God know? Can he judge through the deep darkness?" (Jb 22:13).

"Oh, that I were as in the months of old, as in the days when God watched over me; when his lamp shone upon my head, and by his light I walked through darkness" (Jb 29:2-3).

Author's comment: Note the striking similarity of the faithful's protection from darkness through "God's lamp" with that of the blessed candles mentioned by the prophets and seers in recent times.

"When I waited for light, darkness came" (Jb 30:26).

Author's comment: Note how this resembles the private prophecy given by Marie-Julie Jahenny of Coyault, France: "In the houses of the godless they will not give light."

"He sent darkness, and made the land dark" (Ps 105:28).

Author's comment: Again we see that God has sent His darkness to cover the earth. This same punishment is echoed in the words of Blessed Anna Maria Taigi: "There shall come over all the earth an intense darkness lasting three days and three nights."

"The way of the wicked is like deep darkness; they do not know over what they stumble" (Prv 4:19).

"His lamp will be put out in utter darkness" (Prv 20:20). Author's comment: We see another similar prophecy to those mentioned by various modern seers - the fact that the wicked will not be able to keep any artificial light lit during the three days darkness.

"While over those men alone heavy night was spread, an image of the darkness that was destined to receive them" (Wis 17:21).

Author's comment: It is interesting to note that in the Revised Standard Version Bible, Catholic Edition, the guide words at the top of the page describe the theme of this chapter as "the plague of darkness." This description is similar to the "plague" and "scourge" described by the modern seers already cited.

"And they will look to the earth, but behold, distress and darkness, the gloom of anguish; and they will be thrust into thick darkness" (Is 8:22).

"The people who walk in darkness have seen a great light; those who dwelt in a land of deep darkness, on them has light shined" (Is 9:2).

Author's comment: God's light of grace shines upon the faithful so that they might see, while others remain in darkness. This theme is re-echoed in the voices of the modern seers, who claim that it is through blessed candles that the faithful will see through the three days darkness still to come.

"I form light and create darkness, I make weal and create woe, I am the Lord, who do all these things" (Is 45:7).

Author's comment: Although man creates his own darkness and freely chooses sin, nevertheless it is clear in Sacred Scripture that God Himself at times sends the darkness over humanity. This is how the three days darkness will occur, according to the seers.

"He has driven and brought me into darkness without any light" (Lam 3:2).

"All the bright lights of heaven will I make dark over you, and put darkness upon your land, says the Lord God" (Ez 32:8). "For the day of the Lord is coming, it is near, a day of darkness and gloom, a day of clouds and thick darkness!" (J12:1-2). "'And on that day,' says the Lord God, 'I will make the sun go down at noon, and darken the earth in broad daylight'" (Am 8:9).

"Therefore it shall be night to you, without vision, and darkness to you, without divination. The sun shall go down upon the prophets, and the day shall be black over them" (Mi 3:6).

"A day of wrath is that day, a day of distress and anguish, a day of ruin and devastation, a day of darkness and gloom, a day of clouds and thick darkness" (Zep 1:15).

Author's comment: This prophetic text of Sacred Scripture is describing the "day of the Lord." Some scholars feel that these prophecies were beginning to occur as they were spoken; others feel that they were fulfilled with Israel's destruction by Rome (A.D. 67-70 and A.D. 132); still others believe that the "day of the Lord" refers to a future time that shortly precedes the Second Coming of Christ.

"And in the last days it shall be, God declares, that I will pour out my Spirit upon all flesh, and your sons and your daughters shall prophesy, and your young men shall see visions, and your old men shall dream dreams...And I will show wonders in the heaven above and signs on the earth beneath, blood, and fire, and vapor of smoke; the sun shall be turned into darkness and the moon into blood, before the day of the Lord comes, the great and manifest day" (Acts 2:17,19-20).

"The fourth angel blew his trumpet, and a third of the sun was struck, and a third of the moon, and a third of the stars, so that a third of their light was darkened; a third of the day was kept from shining, and likewise a third of the night" (Rv 8:12).

"The fifth angel poured his bowl on the throne of the beast, and its kingdom was in darkness; men gnawed their tongues in anguish and cursed the God of heaven for their pain and sores, and did not repent of their deeds" (Rv 16:10-11).

Author's comment: This apocalyptic prophecy from Scripture is very similar to the warnings from the private prophecies of the seers we have read. This is especially true for the images of the demons let loose upon the earth as well as the "pain and sores" that are inflicted upon the faithless people.

The Great Monarch: Private Prophecies

"The Great French Monarch who shall subject all the East shall come around the end of the world" (St. Hippolytus, d. c. 235).

"In the last period Christians will not appreciate the great grace of God who provided a Great Monarch, a long duration of peace, a splendid fertility of the earth" (St. Methodius of Olympus, fourth century).

"There will be a great Pope, who will be most eminent in sanctity and most perfect in every quality. This Pope shall have with him the Great Monarch, a most virtuous man, who shall be a scion of the holy race of the French kings. This Great Monarch will assist the Pope in the reformation of the whole earth. But after some considerable time fervor shall cool, iniquity shall abound, and moral corruption shall become worse than ever, which shall bring upon mankind the last and worst persecution of Antichrist and the end of the world" (St. Caesar of Arles, d. 543).

"He will be the greatest and the last of all Monarchs. After having wisely governed his kingdom, he will go in the end to Jerusalem and will lay down his sceptre and his crown upon the Mount of Olives. Immediately afterwards, Antichrist will come" (Abbot Adso of Montier-en-Der, France, d. 996).

"There will come a German Anti-Pope. Italy and Germany will be sorely troubled. A French King will restore the true Pope" (Abbot Joachim Merlin, thirteenth century).

"Before the Christian churches are renovated and united, God send the Eagle (Great Monarch) who will travel to Rome and bring much happiness and good. The Holy Man (Angelic Pastor?) will bring peace between the clergy and the Eagle and his reign will last for four years" Monk Hilarion, d. 1476).

"This great ruler will restore stolen Church property. Protestantism will cease. This duke will be the most powerful monarch on earth. At a gathering of men noted for piety and wisdom he will, with the aid of the Pope, introduce new rules, and ban the spirit of confusion. Everywhere there will be one fold and one shepherd" (Father Laurence Ricci, S.J., d. 1775).

"God will choose a descendant of Constantine, Pepin, and St. Louis, who has been tried by a long period of disappointment, to come from exile to rule over Europe. He will have the sign of the cross on his breast and besides being a religious man, will be kind, wise, just and powerful. Under him the Catholic religion will spread as never before" (Josefa von Bourg, d. 1807).

"Under his reign the greatest righteousness will be practiced and the earth will bear in overabundance" (Abbe Souffrand, d. 1828).

"A Great Monarch will arise after a period of terrible wars and persecutions in Europe. He will be a Catholic: he will not be German" (Brother Louie Ro , d. 1840).

The Great Pope: Private Prophecies

"The Great Monarch and the great Pope will precede Antichrist. The nations will be at war for four years and a great part of the world will be destroyed. The Pope will go over the sea carrying the sign of Redemption on his forehead. The Great Monarch will come to restore peace and the Pope will share in the victory. Peace will reign on earth" (Werdin d'Otrante, thirteenth century).

"After many long sufferings endured by Christians...a remarkable Pope will be seated on the pontifical throne under the special protection of the angels. Holy and full of gentleness, he shall undo all wrong; he shall recover the estate of the Church, and reunite the exiled temporal rulers. He shall be revered by everybody, and shall recover the kingdom of Jerusalem. He shall unite the Eastern and Western Churches" (Abbot Joachim Merlin, thirteenth century).

"After many tribulations, a Pope shall be elected out of those who survived the persecutions. By his sanctity he will reform the clergy, and the whole world shall venerate the Church for her sanctity, virtue, and perfection" (John of Vatiguerro, thirteenth century).

"Under a holy Pope there will be universal conversion" (Dolciano, fourteenth century).

"Violent hands will be laid on the Supreme Head of the Catholic Church" (Bishop George Michael Wittman, d. 1833).

The Blessed Virgin Mary: Private Prophecies

"In the last times the Lord will especially spread the renown of His Mother: Mary began salvation, and by her intercession it will be concluded. Before the second coming of Christ Mary must, more than ever, shine in mercy, might and grace in order to bring unbelievers into the Catholic Faith. The powers of Mary in the last times over the demons will be very conspicuous" (Venerable Mary of Agreda, d. 1665).

"The power of Mary over all devils will be particularly outstanding in the last period of time. From the east to the from the north to the south, all shall proclaim the holy name of Mary; Mary conceived without original sin, Mary Queen of Heaven and earth" (St. Louis de Montfort, 1673-1716).

"I saw the Blessed Virgin ascend on the Church and spread her mantle over it" (Venerable Anne Catherine Emmerich, 1774-1824).

"Holy women, images of Mary, shall have power to work miracles. After them comes Mary to prepare the place for her Son in His triumphant Church. Behold the Immaculate Conception of the Kingdom of God that precedes the arrival of Jesus Christ...Mary, all powerful, shall change all men into good wheat. All shall be good. The Pharisees will be the last to be converted; the great brigands will arrive beforehand. The Jews who have refused Jesus Christ in his humiliation will acknowledge Him at the glorious arrival of Mary" (Venerable Magdalene Porzat, d. 1850).

"We expect that the Immaculate Virgin and Mother of God, Mary, through her most powerful intercession, will bring...about [the fact] that our holy mother, the Catholic Church, after removal of all obstacles and overcoming of all errors, will gain in influence from day to day among the nations and in all places" (Pope Pius IX, 1846-1878).

"The image of the Immaculate will one day replace the large red star over the Kremlin, but only after a great and bloody trial" (St. Maximilian Kolbe, d. 1941).

"I have come to call the world to conversion for the last time. Later, I will not appear any more on this earth" (The Blessed Virgin Mary to the seers of Medjugorje, Yugoslavia, May 2, 1982).

"I wish to keep on giving you messages as it has never been in history from the beginning of the world" (The Blessed Virgin Mary to Marija Pavlovic, Medjugorje, Yugoslavia, April 4, 1985).

"This century has been marked by my strong presence in your midst and, in order to make it perceptible to all, I have everywhere multiplied my miraculous manifestations" (The Blessed Virgin Mary to Father Stefano Gobbi, February 11, 1988).

"I invite you to renunciation for nine days so that with your help everything I wanted to realize through the secrets I began in

Fatima may be fulfilled" (The Blessed Virgin Mary to Marija Pavlovic, Medjugorje, Yugoslavia, August 25, 1991).

The Blessed Virgin Mary: Sacred Scripture

"The Lord God said to the serpent, I will put enmity between you and the woman, and between your seed and her seed; he shall bruise your head, and you shall bruise his heel" (Gn 3:14-15).

Author's comment: It is clear from the private apocalyptic prophecies that the Blessed Virgin Mary will play an extremely important part at the end of the world and preceding the Second Coming of Christ. Particularly, her intercessory role as the "Mediatrix of All Graces" and "Mother of the Church" as well as her protective grace against the wiles of Satan in the final cosmic battle and ultimate victory of good over evil is stated again and again in the hundreds of private prophecies throughout the history of the Church. Indeed, former Cardinal Joseph Ratzinger once stated that one of the signs of our times is the numerous Marian apparitions that have increased throughout the modern-day world. It is clear that Jesus will defeat Satan-indeed, this is perhaps the most important reason he came upon this earth: "The reason the Son of God appeared was to destroy the works of the devil" (1 Jn 3:8). Yet it is Mary who comes to warn us of this diabolical attack upon all humanity, a reality that must keep us on alert: "Your adversary the devil prowls around like a roaring lion, seeking someone to devour" (1 Pt 5:8).

Let us hear the words of St. John in Revelation about the role of the Blessed Virgin at the end of time - perhaps the single most important piece of Scripture that supports the Marian phenomena of our age.

"And a great portent appeared in heaven, a woman clothed with the sun, with the moon under her feet, and on her head a crown of twelve stars; she was with child and she cried out in her pangs of birth, in anguish for delivery. And another portent appeared in heaven; behold, a great dragon. His tail swept down a third of the stars of heaven, and cast them to the earth. And the dragon stood before the woman who was about to bear a child, that he might devour her child when she brought it forth; she brought forth a male child, one who is to rule all the nations with a rod of iron, ... And when the dragon saw that he had been thrown down to the earth, he pursued the woman who had borne the male child. But the woman was given the two wings of the great eagle that she might fly from the serpent into the wilderness, to the place where she is to be nourished for a time, and times, and half a time...Then the dragon was angry with the woman, and went off to make war on the rest of her offspring, on those who keep the commandments of God and bear testimony to Jesus" (Rv 12:1-5, 13-14, 17).

This twelfth chapter not only gives support to the authenticity of modern-day Marian apparitions and warnings, but it also lends weight to other Marian beliefs as well: the fact that she is the Mother of Jesus (Rv 12:5); that the Blessed Virgin is intimately involved with the rise of Satan's power at the end of time (Rv 12:12, 17); that she of all women has a special "place prepared by God" (Rv 12:6); and that she truly is the Mother of the Church ("Then the dragon...went off to make war on the rest of her offspring" [Rv 12:17; emphasis author's).

Admittedly, some Scripture scholars do not attribute this symbolic story of Satan with the Virgin Mary. It is true that the Mother of God is not named directly in this episode. However, there are numerous scholars who do feel that the "woman clothed with the sun" could be no other than the Blessed Virgin.

After all, who else in Sacred Scripture could be the one who "brought forth a male child, one who is to rule all the nations with a rod of iron" (Rv 12:5) and who "was caught up to God and to his throne" (Rv 12:5)? Is there anyone else in history who brought forth such a man? Was there ever anyone else who has ruled the whole world and who was caught up to God's throne? (No, Elijah and Enoch were not. They were assumed into heaven but not to God's throne-see Hebrews 11:5 and 2 Kings 2:11-12.) And what other woman has ever appeared in Scripture with a crown of stars representing a "Queenship of Heaven" (Rv 12:1)?

These are important questions. For if one dismisses the evidence presented in the Book of Revelation, then one has to believe that some other person other than the Blessed Virgin is fulfilling the symbolic role of the "woman clothed with the sun." Yet who could this be? It is very clear that this woman is not a symbolic creature from heaven nor a pure angelic spirit: Angels cannot bear children (Rv 12:4-5), there has never been a physical "wilderness" in heaven (Rv 12:6) that the woman flees to, spirits do not need "nourishment" as this woman does (Rv 12:6), and the earth could not come to the help of this woman" if she were a mythical creature or a pure angelic spirit from heaven. Besides, no one but a human being could be capable of having "offspring" (Rv 12:17).

So a serious problem remains for doubting Scripture scholars as to the reality of this person. If they do not believe it is the Virgin, then who could it ? To admit that it represents a different human would be to go against the teachings of Scripture about Mary, Jesus, Satan, the demons, St. Michael the Archangel, and one who is near the throne of God (Rv 12:5). In fact, it may even run contrary to the teachings of the faith.

Likewise, if these scholars believe that the symbolic woman is a heavenly spirit, the understanding and teaching of the Church concerning the very nature and essence of pure spirits would challenged.

Of course, the woman could not represent an evil spirit: No evil spirit would battle against Satan (Rv 12:7-9), and no child of Satan could ever remain present at God's throne (Rv 12:5).

Finally, these scholars cannot attempt to sweep it all under the rug by saying that this is a make-believe or symbolic story that has no basis in fact. For if this were so, then they would have to deny the reality of the other teachings inseparably embedded throughout the same chapter: those doctrines dealing with the role of St. Michael, the fall of the evil spirits, etc. In other words, these scholars are placed in an inescapable trap. To deny the reality of the "woman clothed with the sun" as being the Blessed Virgin Mary may pose more problems than it solves!

The End of the Present Age (Private Prophecies)

"Men will surrender to the spirit of the age. They will say that if they had lived in our day, faith would be simple and easy. But in their day, they will say, things are complex; the Church must be brought up to date and made meaningful to the day's problems. When the Church and the world are one, then those days are at hand" (St. Antony the Abbot [also known as Antony of the Desert], 251-356).

"Everywhere there is war! People and nations are pitted against each other. War! War! War! Mourning and death everywhere! Famine over the whole world. The cities are destroyed, the natural elements are set loose, the earthquakes everywhere. Thy Church, O Lord, is torn apart by her own children. One camp is faithful to the fleeing Pontiff, the other is subject to the new government of Rome that has broken the Tiara. But Almighty God will, in His mercy, put an end to this confusion and a new age will begin. Then, said the Spirit, this is the beginning of the End of Time" (Premol, d. 496).

"In the 20th century there will be wars and fury that will last a long time; whole provinces shall be emptied of their inhabitants, and kingdoms shall be thrown into confusion. In many places the land shall be left untilled, and there shall be great slaughters of the upper class. The right hand of the world shall fear the left, and the north shall prevail over the south" (Bishop Christianos Ageda, twelfth century).

"It is said that twenty centuries after the Incarnation of the Word, the Beast in its turn shall become man. About the year 2,000...,Antichrist will reveal himself to the world" (Brother John of the Cleft Rock, d. 1340).

"The beginning of the end shall not come in the 19th century, but in the 20th for sure" (Sister Bouquillion, nineteenth century).

"I, your Mother, through the intercession of the Archangel St. Michael, want to tell you to amend your lives. You are in the last warnings!" (The Blessed Virgin Mary to the four seers of Garabandal, Spain, June 19, 1965).

"The world must find salvation while there is time. Let it pray with fervor. May it have the spirit of faith" (The Blessed Virgin Mary to the seers of Medjugorje, Yugoslavia, November 22,1981).

"These apparitions are the last in the world" (The Blessed Virgin Mary to Vicka Ivankovic, Medjugorje, Yugoslavia, as told to Father Tomislav Vlasic on June 23,1982).

"Hurry to be converted. Do not wait for the great sign. For the unbelievers, it will then be too late to be converted" (The Blessed Virgin Mary in a locution to Jelena Vasilj, seer from Medjugorje, Yugoslavia, April 4, 1983).

"Be converted! It will be too late when the sign comes. Beforehand, several warnings will be given to the world. Have people hurry to be converted. I need your prayers and your penance...I will pray to my Son to spare you the punishment. Be converted without delay. You do not know the plans of God; you will not be able to know them. You do not know what God will send, nor what He will do. Be converted! Be ready for everything" (The Blessed Virgin Mary in a locution to Jelena Vasilj of Medjugorje, Yugoslavia, April 25, 1983).

"Hasten your conversion. Do not await the sign, which has been announced. For those who do not believe, it will be too late" (The Blessed Virgin Mary in a locution to Jelena Vasilj of Medjugorje, Yugoslavia, Spring, 1983).

"You cannot imagine what is going to happen nor what the Eternal Father will send to earth. That is why you must be converted! Renounce everything. Do penance. Express my acknowledgment to all my children who have prayed and fasted. I carryall this to my Divine Son in order to obtain an alleviation of His justice against the sins of mankind" (The Blessed Virgin Mary in a locution to Jelena Vasilj of Medjugorje, Yugoslavia, June 24, 1983).

"Before the visible sign is given to humanity, there will be three warnings to the world. The warnings will be in the form of events on earth. Mirjana will be a witness to them. Ten days before one of the admonitions, Mirjana will notify a priest of her choice. The witness of Mirjana will be a confirmation of the apparitions and a stimulus for the conversion of the world...After the admonitions, the visible sign will appear on the site of the apparitions in Medjugorje for all the world to see. The sign will be given to call people back to faith...The ninth and tenth secrets are serious. They concern chastisement for the sins of the world. Punishment is inevitable, for we cannot expect the whole world to be converted. The punishment can be diminished by prayer and penance, but it cannot be eliminated. Mirjana says that one of the evils that threatened the world, the one contained in the seventh secret, has been averted thanks to prayer and fasting...After the first admonition, the others will follow in a rather short time. Thus, people will have some time for conversion...After the visible sign appears, those who are still alive will have little time for conversion. According to Mirjana, the events predicted by the Blessed Virgin are near" (A message from the Blessed Virgin Mary to Mirjana Dragicevic, Medjugorje, Yugoslavia. as reported to Father Tomislav Vlasic on November 5, 1983, and conveyed to Pope John Paul II by Father Vlasic on December 16, 1983).

"You must warn the Bishop very soon, and the Pope, with respect to the urgent and the great importance of the message for all humanity...The peace of the world is in a state of crisis. Become brothers among you, increase prayer and fasting in order to be saved" (The Blessed Virgin Mary to Marija Pavlovic, Medjugorje, Yugoslavia, November 30, 1983).

"Those who say, 'I do not believe in God,' how difficult it will be for them when they will approach the Throne of God and hear the voice: Enter into Hell" (The Blessed Virgin Mary to the seers of Medjugorje, Yugoslavia, as reported to Father Tomislav Vlasic, October 8, 1985).

"The subject on the certainties of catastrophes comes from false prophets. They say, on such a day, at such an hour, there will be a catastrophe. I have always said: Punishment will come about, if the world is not converted. Call all mankind to conversion.

Everything depends on your conversion" (The Blessed Virgin Mary in a locution to Jelena Vasilj, Medjugorje, Yugoslavia, 1986).

The End of the Present Age: Sacred Scripture

"In many and various ways God spoke of old to our fathers by the prophets; but in these last days he has spoken to us by a Son, whom he appointed the heir of all things, through whom also he created the world" (Heb 1:1-2).

"For many will come in my name, saying, 'I am the Christ,' and they will lead many astray. And you will hear of wars and rumors of wars; see that you are not alarmed; for this must take place, but the end is not yet. For nation will rise against nation, and kingdom against kingdom, and there will be famines and earthquakes in various places: all this is but the beginning of the sufferings" (Mt 24:5-8).

"Immediately after the tribulation of those days the sun will be darkened, and the moon will not give its light, and the stars will fall from heaven, and the powers of the heavens will be shaken" (Mt 24:29).

"From the fig tree learn its lesson: as soon as its branch becomes tender and puts forth its leaves, you know that summer is near. So also, when you see all these things, you know that he is near, at the very gates. Truly, I say to you, this generation will not pass away till all these things take place. Heaven and earth will pass away, but my words will not pass away" (Mt 24:32-35).

The Second Coming of Christ: Private Prophecies

"The world will see the Lord coming upon the clouds of heaven" (Didache, 90-100).

"God will come again, though armed: then will all see that He is the Lord of this world, created by Him, out of which they tried to expel Him" (Bishop Pie of Portiers, d. 1880).

"Before I come as a just judge I will reveal Myself as the King of Mercy so that no one will be able to excuse himself on the Day of Judgment which is slowly approaching" (Jesus to Sister Faustina Kowalska in Poland, 1905-1938).

"I tell you truly, the time has come for the world to repent, for a universal change is near, such as has never been from the beginning of the world until this day: and will never be again" (Madeleine of Dozule, France, 1974).

"Mary has come to prepare the world for the return of her Son. . .We have to suffer with Jesus, to pray and be apostles for His return" (Alphonsine, a visionary from Kibeho, Africa, 1981).

The Second Coming of Christ: Sacred Scripture

"For as the lightning comes from the east and shines as far as the west, so will be the coming of the Son of man" (Mt 24:27).

"But of that day and hour no one knows, not even the angels of heaven, nor the Son, but the Father only...Watch therefore, for you do not know on what day your Lord is coming. Therefore, you also must be ready; for the Son of man is coming at an hour you do not expect...Watch therefore, for you know neither the day nor the hour" (Mt 24:36, 42, 44; 25:13).

"As were the days of Noah, so will be the coming of the Son of man. For as in those days before the flood they were eating and drinking, marrying and giving in marriage, until the day when Noah entered the ark, and they did not know until the flood came and swept them all away, so will be the coming of the Son of man" (Mt 24:37-39).

"When the Son of man comes in his glory, and all the angels with him, then he will sit on his glorious throne" (Mt 25:31).

"And then they will see the Son of man coming in a cloud with power and great glory. Now when these things begin to take place, look up and raise your heads, because your redemption is drawing near" (Lk 21:27-28).

About the Author

My background as a publisher author is wide and diverse. Here is a general bibliography of my works and the television shows I have appeared on concerning some of those works:

The nationally-published books to my credit:

"Questions And Answers: The Gospel of Matthew"

"Questions And Answers: The Gospel of Mark"

"Questions And Answers: The Gospel of Luke"

"Questions And Answers: The Gospel of John"

(All published with Baker Book House of Grand Rapids, MI).

On the more scholarly side, I have written the following works:

"They Bore The Wounds Of Christ: The Mystery Of The Sacred Stigmata"

"The Making Of Saints"

"Voices, Visions, & Apparitions"

"Patron Saints"

(All published with Our Sunday Visitor of Huntington, IN).

One of my recent eBooks now in print with Amazon Kindle ("The Complete Guide To Demonology & The Spirits of Darkness") received the Imprimatur after a prior review by the former Bishop

Elden Curtiss of the Diocese of Helena, Montana. Released in December 2015, it is 450 pages long.

My Self-Published Religious eBooks In Print

My eBooks with Amazon Kindle:

"Demonology & The Spirits of Darkness: History Of Demons" (Volume 1: 184 pages)

"Demonology & The Spirits of Darkness: The Spiritual Warfare" (Volume 2: 135 pages)

"Demonology & The Spirits of Darkness: Possession & Exorcism" (Volume 3: 127 pages)

"Demonology & The Spirits of Darkness: Dictionary of Demonology" (Volume 4: 252 pages)

"Demonology & The Spirits of Darkness: A Catholic Perspective" (Volume 5: 450 pages)

"Demonology & The Spirits of Darkness: Infestation, Oppression, & Demonic Activity" (Volume 6: 130 pages)

"Demonology & The Spirits of Darkness: History Of The Occult" (Volume 7: 70 pages)

"Demonology & The Spirits of Darkness: Witchcraft & Sorcery" (Volume 8: 93 pages)

"Demonology & The Spirits of Darkness: Evil Spirits In The Bible" (Volume 9: 43 pages)

"Demonology & The Spirits of Darkness: The Exorcist" (Volume 10: 95 pages)

"Demonology & The Spirits of Darkness: Types Of Demons & Evil Spirits" (Volume 11: 89 pages)

"Demonology & The Spirits of Darkness: Temptations Of The Devil" (Volume 12: 48 pages)

"Voices, Visions, & Apparitions: Voices From Heaven" (Volume 1, 25 pages)

"Voices, Visions, & Apparitions: Heaven, Hell, & Purgatory" (Volume 2, 25 pages)

"Ghosts Poltergeists and Haunting Spirits: A Religious Perspective" (141 pages)

"The Mystery of the Sacred Stigmata: My Interviews With Padre Pio's Spiritual Advisors" (Volume 1, 25 pages)

"The Mystery of the Sacred Stigmata: My Personal Interview With The Vice Postulator For The Cause Of Beatification Of Therese Neumann" (Volume 2, 29 pages)

"Voices, Visions, & Apparitions: Heaven, Hell, & Purgatory" (25 pages)

"Voices, Visions, & Apparitions: Voices From Heaven" (33 pages)

"Voices, Visions, & Apparitions: Angels & Saints" (46 pages)

"Angels In The Bible: The Bible Trivia Series" (Volume 1) (52 pages)

"The Gospel of Matthew: The Bible Trivia Series (Volume 2)" (127 pages)

"The Gospel of Matthew: The Bible Trivia Series (Volume 3)" (147 pages)

"1,130 Bible Trivia Questions! The Bible Trivia Series (Volume 4)" (242 pages)

"30 Christmas Poems To Make Your Holidays Bright!: Special Poems For The Holiday Season" (32 pages)

"300 Christmas Trivia Facts You Might Not Know!: Customs, Traditions, Celebrations" (18 pages)

"Do You Really Know Jesus Christ? Questions About The Biblical Jesus" (104 pages)

Educational Background

A Bachelor of Arts degree in Secondary Education from the University of Montana, Missoula, Montana (1984). My major is English with minors in Religious Studies & History.

Television Appearances

Television Appearances as a guest interviewee for my works: "The History Channel," "The Phil Donahue Show," "The Leeza Show," and "EWTN: Mother Angelica Live!" (3 times as a guest).

My YouTube Videos For My National National Appearances

As A Guest Interviewee For My Books

https://www.youtube.com/channel/UCmrULjCTF4ljSLwynLYO3fQ

Links To My Writing Sites

http://www.amazon.com/-/e/B001KIZJS4

https://www.facebook.com/mike.freze1

Made in United States
Troutdale, OR
01/30/2025

28512615R00050